Let's Explore

Earth

Helen and David Orme

GARETH**STEVENS**

PUBLISHING

A Member of the WRC Media Family of Companies

Please visit our web site at: www.garethstevens.com
For a free color catalog describing Gareth Stevens Publishing's list
of high-quality books and multimedia programs, call
1-800-542-2595 (USA) or 1-800-387-3178 (Canada).
Gareth Stevens Publishing's fax: (414) 332-3567.

Library of Congress Cataloging-in-Publication Data

Orme, Helen.
Let's explore Earth / Helen and David Orme. — North American ed.
   p. cm. — (Space launch!)
Includes index.
ISBN-13: 978-0-8368-7939-1 (lib. bdg.)
ISBN-13: 978-0-8368-8124-0 (softcover)
1. Earth—Juvenile literature. I. Orme, David, 1948 Mar. 1- II. Title.
QB631.4.O76   2007
550—dc22   2006034713

This North American edition first published in 2007 by
Gareth Stevens Publishing
A Member of the WRC Media Family of Companies
330 West Olive Street, Suite 100
Milwaukee, Wisconsin 53212 USA

This U.S. edition copyright © 2007 by Gareth Stevens, Inc. Original edition copyright © 2006 by ticktock Entertainment Ltd. First published in Great Britain in 2006 by ticktock Media Ltd., Unit 2, Orchard Business Centre, North Farm Road, Tunbridge Wells, Kent, TN2 3XF, United Kingdom.

The publishers would like to thank: Sandra Voss, Tim Bones, James Powell, Indexing Specialists (UK) Ltd.

ticktock project editor: Julia Adams
ticktock project designer: Emma Randall

Gareth Stevens Editorial Direction: Mark Sachner
Gareth Stevens Editors: Barbara Kiely Miller and Carol Ryback
Gareth Stevens Art Direction: Tammy West
Gareth Stevens Designer: Dave Kowalski

Photo credits (t=top, b=bottom, c=center, l=left, r=right, bg=background)
CORBIS: 15bl, 21tl; NASA: 13bl, 21br; Science Photo Library: 4–5bg (original); Shutterstock: front cover, 1, 3bg, 8b, 9tl, 9tr, 9cr, 9br, 11b, 12b, 16c, 18b, 19bl, 22cl; ticktock picture archive: 5tr, 6bl, 6–7bg, 7tr, 7b, 10bl, 10–11bg, 11tl, 13tr, 14bl, 14–15bg, 15tr, 17tr, 17bl, 17br, 18–19bg, 19tr, 20c, 22cr, 22–23bg, 23tl, 23bl, 23br. Rocket drawing Dave Kowalski/© Gareth Stevens, Inc.

Printed in Canada

1 2 3 4 5 6 7 8 9 10 10 09 08 07 06

Contents

Words in the glossary are printed in **bold** the first time they appear in the text.

Where is Earth?

There are eight known planets in our **solar system**. The planets travel around the Sun. Earth is the third planet from the Sun.

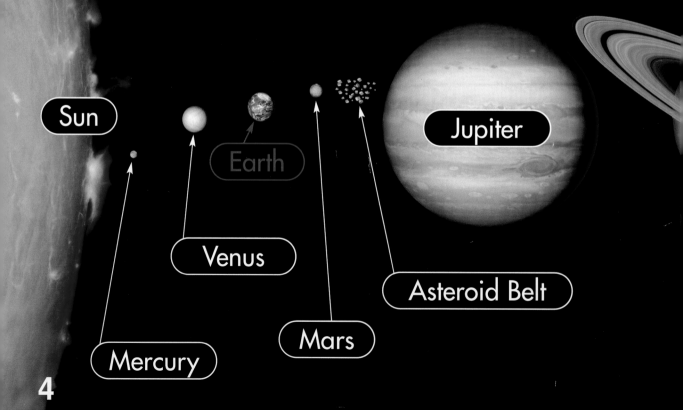

Sun

Earth

Jupiter

Venus

Asteroid Belt

Mars

Mercury

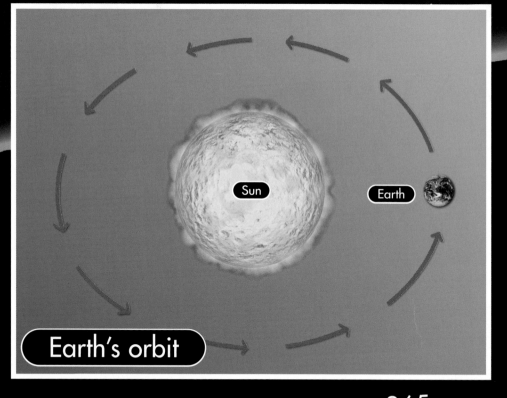

Earth's orbit

Earth travels around the Sun once every 365 days. This journey around the Sun is called Earth's **orbit**. The time a planet takes to orbit the Sun once is called a year.

Saturn

Uranus

Neptune

Pluto

Kuiper Belt

Planet Facts

Earth is the only known planet in our solar system with **liquid** water on its surface. More than three-quarters of our planet is covered by water.

Planets are always spinning. A day is the time it takes a planet to spin around once. One day on Earth is 24 hours long.

direction of spin

7,926 miles
(12,750 kilometers)

The blue areas are water.

The brown areas are land.

The white areas are clouds.

Earth

daytime

nighttime

This artwork shows that, as Earth spins, one half of the planet faces away from the Sun. This half is in the dark. The other half of Earth has sunlight.

Earth has two places called poles — the North Pole and the South Pole. They are at the top and bottom of the planet. The Sun does not shine very strongly at the poles, so they are cold and icy all year.

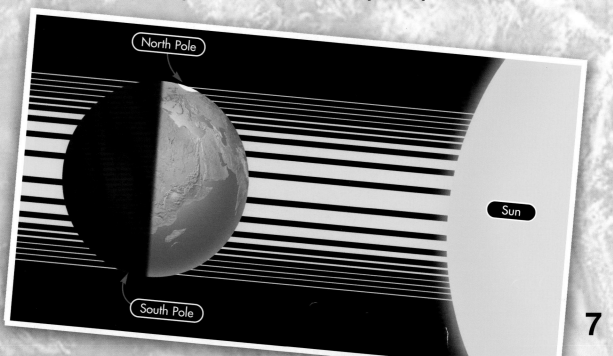

North Pole

Sun

South Pole

Life on Earth

Earth is the only planet we know about where people, animals, and plants can live. Life is possible on Earth because it has liquid water.

The most important thing needed for life is water. But Earth is perfect for life in other ways, too.

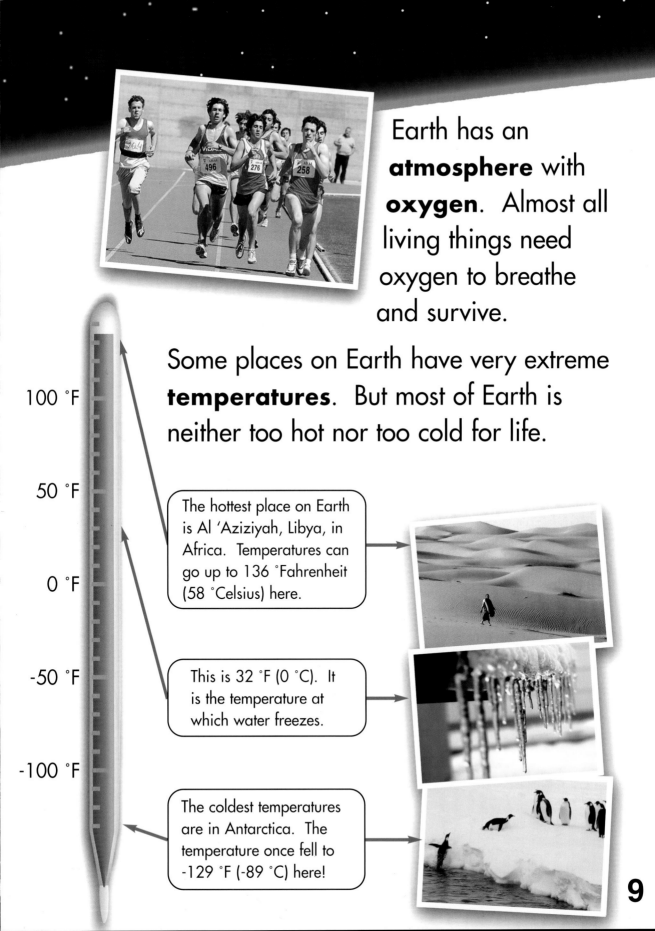

Earth has an **atmosphere** with **oxygen**. Almost all living things need oxygen to breathe and survive.

Some places on Earth have very extreme **temperatures**. But most of Earth is neither too hot nor too cold for life.

100 °F

50 °F

0 °F

-50 °F

-100 °F

The hottest place on Earth is Al 'Aziziyah, Libya, in Africa. Temperatures can go up to 136 °Fahrenheit (58 °Celsius) here.

This is 32 °F (0 °C). It is the temperature at which water freezes.

The coldest temperatures are in Antarctica. The temperature once fell to -129 °F (-89 °C) here!

What's the Weather Like?

The layer of gases that make up Earth's atmosphere is called air. Air covers the planet. Because air moves around, we have different sorts of weather in different places.

When the air moves, we have wind. The wind can be very powerful. Along with water, the wind has given this rock a strange shape by wearing it away over many years.

Strong winds can cause a lot of damage to buildings and trees.

Wind also moves clouds around the planet. Clouds are made up of millions of very tiny water droplets. These droplets can join together to make bigger drops. If these drops become big and heavy enough, they fall from the clouds as rain.

11

Changing Temperatures

Earth is perfect for life, because it is not too hot or too cold. But scientists think that the temperatures on Earth are changing.

smoke with carbon dioxide

When we burn oil or coal, we make a gas called **carbon dioxide**. The amount of this gas in our atmosphere is growing.

Carbon dioxide trapped in our planet's atmosphere stops heat from escaping from Earth. Scientists think that the trapped gases will slowly make Earth heat up.

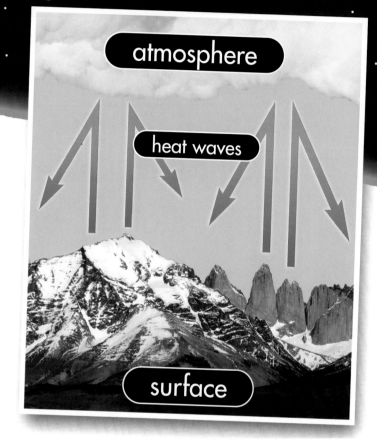

atmosphere

heat waves

surface

Temperature change has already happened on the planet Venus. This planet has heated up so much that it is much too hot and dry for life.

Earth's Crust

Planet Earth is a huge ball of rock. It is made up of four layers. The center of Earth is called its core. The inside of the planet is very hot.

Earth has an inner core and an outer core. The inner core is the hottest part of Earth. Both cores are mainly made of **iron**.

This layer is the mantle. It is made of red-hot rock. Some of it is **molten rock**.

The crust of Earth is the part that we live on. It is made up of land and oceans. It floats on top of the mantle.

inside Earth

Earth's crust is split into sections called **plates**. The plates are moving very slowly all the time.

The red lines on this map show the edges of the plates. They fit together like a giant jigsaw puzzle!

Sometimes, when the plates move, the earth shakes so much that the ground shudders and cracks or lifts up. We call this an earthquake.

Earth's surface is covered with mountains and valleys. The highest mountain on Earth is Mount Everest. It is 29,035 feet (8,850 meters) high!

Mount Everest is so high, its top is sometimes higher than the clouds!

Mountains are made by the movement of Earth's plates. When two plates push against each other, they sometimes create a mountain by pushing layers of rock up. Mount Everest was created this way, but it takes millions of years for this to happen.

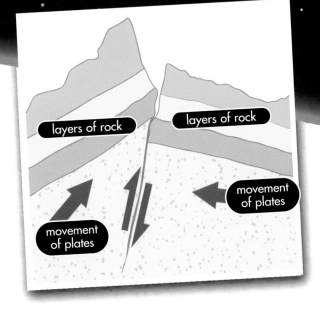

layers of rock

layers of rock

movement of plates

movement of plates

molten rock

volcano

plates

Sometimes when the plates move, an opening appears in Earth's crust. The hot molten rock inside Earth bursts to the surface. The place where this happens is called a volcano.

The Moon and Satellites

The Moon is a huge rock that orbits Earth. Objects that orbit a planet are called **satellites**. The Moon is Earth's only natural satellite.

As seen from Earth, the Moon is the brightest object in the solar system after the Sun. We can see it without using a telescope.

satellite being launched on a rocket

Earth has many other satellites. These satellites have been launched into space on rockets. They have many different uses.

satellite orbiting Earth

Satellites are used to show television programs and connect cell phone calls. Some satellites can give us information about Earth's weather and warn us about **hurricanes**.

Earth in History

Hundreds of years ago, most people believed that the world was flat. They believed that you could fall off the edge of the world!

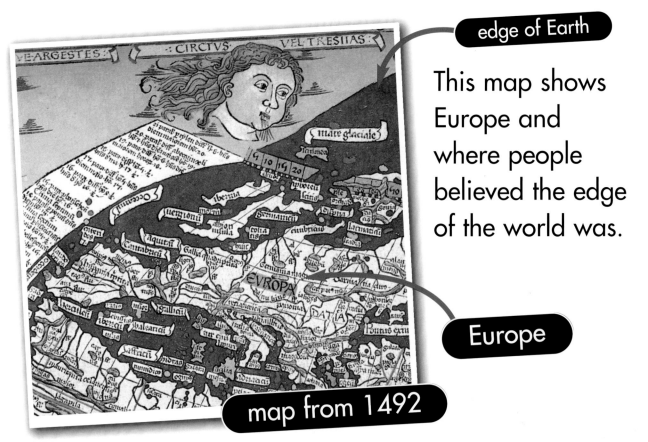

edge of Earth

This map shows Europe and where people believed the edge of the world was.

Europe

map from 1492

When **astronomers** saw the other planets were round, they realized that Earth had to be round, too.

Earth

Sun

People also used to think that the Sun traveled around Earth. Today we know it is the other way around.

This picture was painted in 1660, more than 300 years ago. It shows the Sun orbiting Earth.

With space travel and the help of satellites, we can see that Earth is round and that it orbits the Sun. This photograph of Earth was taken in 1968 by **astronauts** orbiting the Moon.

Moon's surface

Exploring Earth

We still don't know everything there is to know about Earth. Satellites and robots can help us learn more about our planet.

Sahara Desert

Satellites can take photographs of wide areas of land. These photographs help us make very exact maps of large regions of Earth. They also let us see what Earth looks like from space.

Robots can be used to explore and take pictures of the deepest parts of the ocean.

Some robots look for **oil** and **minerals** on the ocean floor.

Some robots can study animals that live in the deepest oceans, such as this fish.

Glossary

asteroid a rocky object that orbits the Sun. Most asteroids orbit the Sun between Mars and Jupiter.

astronauts people trained to travel or work in space

astronomers people who study outer space, often using telescopes

atmosphere the gases that surround a planet, moon, or star

carbon dioxide a gas that is made when something burns

hurricanes the largest, strongest storms on Earth. They form over an ocean, and their high winds spin in a circle.

iron a very hard and strong metal

liquid something that flows and pours easily

minerals material from the earth that is not a plant or an animal. Gold, silver, iron, and salt are all minerals.

molten rock rock that has been melted and flows like a liquid

oil a greasy liquid that many machines need in order to work

orbit the path that a planet or other object takes when traveling around the Sun, or the path a satellite takes around a planet

oxygen one of the gases in Earth's atmosphere that we breathe. People and animals need oxygen to live.

plates the separate pieces that make up Earth's crust. They float very slowly over liquid rock.

satellites moons or man-made objects that are in orbit around a planet

solar system the Sun and everything that is in orbit around it

temperatures how hot or cold things are

Index